the patience of i

the patience of ice

renate wood

TRIQUARTERLY BOOKS
NORTHWESTERN UNIVERSITY PRESS
EVANSTON, ILLINOIS

TriQuarterly Books

Northwestern University Press

Evanston, Illinois 60208-4210

Grateful acknowledgment is made to the editors of the following periodicals, in which these poems first appeared, sometimes in slightly different form: *Many Mountains Moving* ("If She Could Forget Her Mourning," "My Mother's Hair," "Song of Forgetting," "Still Life," "What Is Mourning Made Of?" [formerly titled "Season"]); *Marlboro Review* ("Helen"); *Meridian* ("Absence," "Bullet: 1944," "Medals: 1945," "The Radio: 1944" [all from "German Chronicle"]); *Ploughshares* ("Berlin: 1940/1945," "Cigarette Case: 1942," "Cut Photograph: 1941," "Eels: 1943," "Five Thousand Head of Cattle: 1944," "My Father's Tailor: 1943," [all from "German Chronicle"]); *Seneca Review* ("Erigone," "The Patience of Ice," "Walking: 1948," "White Birds" [formerly titled "Waving"]); *TriQuarterly* ("Black Hat," "My Mother's Hand Thinks," "The Nightgown"); and *Virginia Quarterly Review* ("The Dump," "Eurydice," "Night Cows").

Printed in the United States of America

ISBN 0-8101-5104-9 (cloth)

ISBN 0-8101-5105-7 (paper)

Library of Congress Cataloging-in-Publication Data

Wood, Renate, 1938–

    The patience of ice / Renate Wood.

    p. cm.

    ISBN 0-8101-5104-9 (cloth : alk. paper) — ISBN 0-8101-5105-7 (paper : alk. paper)

    I. Title.

    PS3573.O596P37 2000

    811'.54—dc21

                                                                00-010457

The paper used in this publication meets the minimum requirements of the American National Standard for Information Sciences—Permanence of Paper for Printed Library Materials, ANSI Z39.48-1984.

For Bill,
for Oliver and Chris

contents

part four

acknowledgments

My thanks extend to the Colorado Council on the Arts for its generous support through a 1995 CoVisions Recognition Award.

To Reg Gibbons, for his faith in this book and his keen eye, my very special thanks.

This book wouldn't have been completed without the insight and encouragement of Joan Aleshire, Ellen Greenhouse, Susan Kolodny, Marilyn Krysl, Joy Manesiotis, Debra Nystrom, Moira Powers, Ellen Bryant Voigt, and, especially, Bill Wood. My gratitude to all.

I am also indebted to Amy Schroeder for her attentive editorial support.

part one

German Chronicle

You can't abandon me
now when I'm dead and need tenderness.
—Zbigniew Herbert

1. Cut Photograph: 1941

My mother cared most about beauty. Its absence
hurt her like sickness, like loss of life.
So she cut the photograph at that place on my father's chest
below the heart where the belly begins, leaving intact
my body, riding his shoulders, and his arms
stretched out above his tanned grin, holding my hands in his hands.
A band of sky and sea behind us—bereft of pounded shells and sand
where we'd been walking—we floated then, relieved
of beach and history with its brutal endings.
For years in the plastic window of my wallet
I carried this proof that beauty lives,
something clipped out of a tangled story and freed,
a world of its own, complete with its own plot:
the tiny rider lifting a man out of the sea
where he is half submerged. She's pulling him firmly,
her legs slung around his neck: at any moment now
he will emerge, dripping down to his ankles,
and they'll float higher into the cloudless day.

2. Cigarette Case: 1942

When I think of them now, those men
drafted to work for a war they didn't believe in,
I see their gray suits arriving at our house after dark,
hands buried in their pockets. Once the door to my father's room
closed, with the flick of one hand they opened
those sleek silver cases filled with the slim wrapped shapes,

miniature corpses lined up in a row, lit them
all over the room like small funeral pyres, saying some things
aloud and others in whispers—and I, in my father's lap,
crying into his big white handkerchief about my first
pulled tooth, watched as if I already knew
that men can be extracted and leave a space, not only gaping
but blank and dismissive: a lid clicked shut for good—
They knew their turn would come, being not only tools
but targets. They waited and watched the smoke unfurl
across their faces, still young and eager—
Even the spy in their midst was only a man who wanted to live.

3. Eels: 1943

On the Sundays when they emptied the wicker traps
the men would enter the kitchen. Their rubber boots
tracked across the tiles and left them streaked and smeary.
Some brought buckets of salt, some the heavy tubs
of muscled mass, thick as a man's arm, but pliable
as rope and slimy: too slippery for bare hands.
My father with his friends would frost his palms
with salt before he'd lift each dangling beast
and rub down its length of blackish skin.
They scrubbed and rinsed them. They mopped the floor.
But even when they'd driven off to the smokehouse
a sickening smell stayed and trapped our breath.
From the bottom of one tub the cut-off heads would glint
like cold steel buttons on military leather.

4. My Father's Tailor: 1943

His hands at home in yards of fabric,
woolens, flannel, and fine cotton; they were so nimble
he could fix anything. His vests were famous.
He knew how to shape fabric as if it were clay,

as if he could fashion the man himself. And he could tell
the latest gossip in the city of Riga,
holding five pins in the left corner of his mouth.
The last time he came to the apartment
a guard stayed by the door with a gun,
and while he fixed the stove in our kitchen
I watched my mother stuff cigarettes and bread
    into his baggy pockets.
Her hands were trembling. No words were said.
And after he was gone, she cried
over the little gas wreaths of bluish flame.

5. *Five Thousand Head of Cattle: 1944*

In some history Baltic refugees recorded,
my father is acknowledged for rescuing
five thousand head of cattle overrun by the eastern front.
Whom else he might have helped or counseled—or
whom he failed—is not recorded, nor what he said or thought.
But there are five thousand cows that made it, thanks to him,
onto a freight train heading west. When I think of them
and their descendants, grazing somewhere near
what was Danzig once or Prussia,
they lift their heads to pause as they chew,
not caring whether they're Polish or German,
and look east with their big dreamy eyes—
then bow their heads down to the grass.

6. *Bullet: 1944*

When he aimed his revolver, we stood halfway
behind him and held our breath before the still, white hand
with its finger on the trigger. Then we counted the echoes
answering back through the winter night
and touched the wound in the tree where the bullet

had buried itself like a secret grief.
It was his last visit.
We'd coaxed him long enough, a handful of children
walking home through woods more silent now
than they had been. Much later I saw he'd wanted
to please us. Then I wondered whether that tree still stood
somewhere in Austria, if I could still find it. There are moments
when I see myself reaching into the splintered wood
to feel its metal core. Every time,
it singes my finger to the bone.

7. The Radio: 1944

Nobody could remember how he had carried it or why
it hadn't been confiscated, a handsome Blaupunkt
with foreign names printed on the dial's backlit glass
where the needle would wander from Belgrade to Hilversum,
London, and Paris. From the unlit station of some Alpine village
he pulled it on a sled up the mountain. That's how I see him:
a man alone in the snow under stars glinting like distant cities,
his gaze traveling among them as if to ask: Is there
a place to go where one could live? In our room
when we unpacked it the glass was broken, and my mother
assembled the shards like a puzzle. On tracing paper
she copied the cities as bright dots and cut a hole
for the dial knob. Fitted into the walnut frame of the casing
it covered the void that gaped behind the needle,
holding the shattered world in place.

8. Berlin: 1940/1945

I remember nothing of that city but a dead mouse
we buried together, how my mother scooped out a hole
in my grandfather's garden and I placed the small corpse
inside, wrapped in its shroud of maple leaf.

How I filled in the earth until it made a mound
and marked it with a small oval of stones.
Later when we found out about my father,
how he had died in that city, I remembered
that mouse and how my mother had wiped the earth from the ring
on her finger so carefully. Then I saw that soil
on the ring of his hand. And he and the mouse
became inseparable, so when I thought of him walking through the
    streets
in those last days, there was always a mouse on the sidewalk
scampering ahead like a shadow before him.

9. Cherry Soup: 1945

During a lull two weeks before the end, my father
visited the landlady of his student days in Berlin.
A soldier now, soiled with the grime of trenches and history,
he knocked at her house in the midst of ruins. The first thing
she remembered was his adoration of her sweet cherry soup.
Though bad knees and air raids had slowed the last harvest,
it had been a good year for cherries, and her preserves
were still lined up in the basement next to her makeshift bed.
While he sat by the boarded kitchen window, she scooped out
the thickened juice dotted with fruit, and they talked
of years that had been innocent and sweet—
Behind the window boards the cherry blossoms listened one more
    time.

10. Medals: 1945

There weren't many, perhaps three or four,
for services in the Ministry of Food.
His dissertation I still keep unread on my shelf:
the breeding and raising of pigs in Great Britain.
Did his study improve the production of German pork?

Or was he by then concerned with cabbage crops and cattle?
What does a country eat during war but cruelty and grief?

My mother kept them in a small box I'd never seen
until the late spring after the snowmelt
and before the occupation. After we walked in the woods
where, with a spoon, we dug a hole under layers of pine needles,
she lifted the lid and let us hold each one of them:
one was enameled, one silver, one had a colored ribbon.
Why couldn't we keep them? Why couldn't we have them
to play with? My sister and I still argued with her while we patted
the soil and moss back in place.

For a long time we had no news.
Later it seemed we had buried him then.

11. Shame

Children have their own cruelty.
I wanted him to have rescued five thousand men.
I wanted him to have resisted openly, to be hammered in stone.
I wanted his goodness mounted for all to see.
Children want desperately so much
because so little is left of a man who was human.

12. Absence

It is not nothing. Not the cottonwood felled
in the yard, its split trunk hauled away; not
the stump that stayed behind, its white circle ringed with bark—
but those far-reaching branches built on air
that sway and spread as if the mind had its own wind and light:
the ghosts of birds fly through it.

Walking: 1948

For years she would recognize the broad back under the raincoat,
the wisps of straight blond hair combed sideways,
and his step—one foot turned slightly inward—
his step that came from another time, when, from the swing's
wild height, she'd spot her father turning down the alley
along the garden fence: his face ambling closer, a smile
more in the eyes than at the mouth. Distance, they knew,
was dense with thickets . . . Someone missing
could not be the same as someone gone:
walking behind this man, as the rain dripped
from his upturned collar and soaked in at the back seams,
she craved only this street, the pavement's
bloom so thick it made her dizzy.

But another kind of knowing brewed: as if you walked up
to a fence, opened and closed the gate behind you,
and now there was just this one space *inside*
from which all *outside* had been sliced away—
such singularity, such terrifying lack . . .

part two

My Mother's Hair

The very old do not succumb to disease—
they implode their way into eternity.
—Sherwin B. Nuland, *How We Die*

It's not fall yet, the wind says, but spills a few yellow leaves
onto the grass. It whispers with a thousand voices:
I will be back, and back, and the third time I come

I'll bring your mother's snowy hair. In a far country
my mother's head bobs through a hallway with many doors,
and each is strange. *I've lost my daughter.*

Her name is Renate. Do you know her? she says,
as someone dressed in white comes by to do her hair,
pale halo of the dying, crown of forgetfulness—

I send a picture, knowing I'm thinner now
than those six letters of the alphabet, a nothing
like a single hair brushed off my mother's collar.

Where is the child whose braids she braided, the toddler, the baby?
Erased, as if they went before her like the first yellow leaves
lost in the grass. *My daughter went away,* she says,

it is not right. Families should be together. And far from her,
behind my house, clouds drift across the Rockies.
Each is my mother's hair, fine wool above her forehead.

Over the mesa the wind scatters its wispy skein. The grove of aspen
shivers. Lowering their heads, sunflowers nod, and one by one
the seeds evacuate their sheaths:

one small ellipsis huddled to the next like an old honeycomb,
the brain stem rattling its husks. I pick up
the seed of a cottonwood where it's caught in the grass

and smooth its white tuft until each strand glistens in the sun.
Where are you going? I say, placing it on my palm.
Into the wind, it says, *into the voice of nothing, home of us all.*

Song of Forgetting

You feel your age, you say, your head's not right.
At eighty-six forgetting is easy: things drift away
like down caught on your breath.

You can tell each morning when you fluff the pillows
how many feathers are gone. You're tired
of chasing after what doesn't want to stay.

Clocks, closets, calendars, and places in books you loved
have emptied themselves: the regiment of angels
that used to keep up order there

moved on to another site. What day is today,
you ask on the phone, and as you ask you're tired
of knowing. *Nothing,* you tell me, you want nothing:

the only thing you can't forget.
Later you pick up the piece of linen I sent
and pluck out strands of gray woof from the weave

to form a design of pulled threads.
A band of warp remains, a row of fibrous slats
your needle ties a few at a time into tight bundles

to show what's empty in between—
nothing, invited in: like the still surface of a pond
in which the fish choose not to jump but linger

near the bottom. They forget they're fish and hang
like fruit from watery branches. How you want to be
like them: deep in the world and not knowing it.

Lesson with Butter Cube

All summer I couldn't wash my hands without lifting it
out of my way, that glistening cube which bobbed in a dish
under the dripping faucet. Its surface no longer
neatly squared, but nicked and malleable, a paste—
I could draw with my finger on it
and watch how laws of chemistry and physics made it unable
to submerge itself, even in fiercest heat.
It was the time my mother, suspended in her mourning,
defied submersion into sleep. She only floated in it,
on the surface. When I coughed during the night
she sat straight up in her bed, as if I'd wakened her
from her nonsleep where she was always drifting
without completely drowning—
Grief keeps us so fiercely in this world.

If She Could Forget Her Mourning

I ask myself these days: What if my mother,
who in her old age has forgotten half a world
that spread in her mind like grasses covering the hills,

what if she now forgot her mourning—
her mourning for the dead, the promise of their lives
not kept; her mourning for eighty years

that didn't yield what she'd hoped for,
a harvest spoiled by inclemencies of fate—
what if at last she forgot her losses and woke without saying,

I wasn't lucky? —If she forgot her worries:
first the one about the world's woes and wants,
then the one about sickness

in her loved ones, the one about money, about
being wrinkled and ugly, about not
having been enough?

Would she laugh then before she died—her mind
lighter than dandelions gone to seed—
would she die from the jolt of her laughing?

Black Hat

The nurses say the old ask for bright colored sheets.
They make the days less plain: bold plaids or flowers
absorb the eye. Now that she lies
under the paisley covers I bought, it's hard

to imagine that once for a year she wore a black hat.
Her skin pale as now, Hamburg 1948: the train station
crowded with children returning from Sweden,
late January snow, soot, drafty ruins.

I had been homesick for three months and didn't mind
that hat, nor her chatting with the nurse
from the Red Cross. That night in the hotel room
we huddled close in bed and warmed each other.

Her hat lay turned up on the chair like a black boat.
When she turned off the light, the boat grew in the dark,
grew and began to float. It was then she told me
about my sister, why there had been no letters

for weeks. Black hat, black hat, together
we lay there drifting inside a ship of grief.
Next day at home she took out fresh white sheets
and moved into my sister's bed. The hat hung on the nail

behind the kitchen door. When we went out she wore it.
Nights in my sister's covers for years she never slept.
And when I drifted into sleep in my own separate bed
I saw her pushing off into her sleepless world

waving high from the deck of a black steamer,
my sister wrapped tight in her arm. Black hat, white sheets,
how they keep coming back: smokestacks and snow—
But it is summer now and I have brought new linens

printed with tiny rosebuds. The nurses ooh and aah
as I unwrap them, and my mother, who now mostly sleeps,
lifts her lids just a bit and stares for a moment,
as if those buds might open.

What Is Mourning Made Of?

There were years when it was always winter:
the birds laid eggs in nests of snow
and cherry trees grew petals of iced lace.

My mother wore a suit of black, her lips were blue,
her eyes frozen over. I did my homework
in wool mittens, scraping an icicle across the blue-gray slate,

a language of thin ribbons erasing itself. But the starched
black ribbons of my braids looped like sad letters
and stayed in my hair. What is mourning made of?

Some say it's cold, some say it's black, some say
it's salt—the salt in all you eat, the salt
you become, like Lot's wife who couldn't take

her eyes from the city burning. But I remember
the story of a child who carried a heavy pitcher—
a dead child burdened with her mother's tears.

Stop crying, the child said, *this is too much to carry.*
Yet in my story it's the living child who says
Stop crying, and after she is punished she does not

speak again. On the walls of the house hang portraits
of the dead. Each on its own nail. Each dusted
every day. And the living child stands by the window.

Through the glass she watches the bees, their dusty
golden bodies lifting out of the petaled cups:
Drink, they say, *sweet drink.*

But the child sees only the tiny head,
pointed and dipping, like hurt, like greed,
like stealing what isn't yours.

White Birds

Each morning we'd wave to each other at the exact moment
when her slim figure would appear on the sidewalk of the next
        block
where a gap between row houses, perhaps of fifteen steps or so,

opened a view from our upstairs window. Each day,
after she left for work and before I left for school,
I'd wait by that window to catch a glimpse of her

across the distance and the debris of the bombed building
that made a vacant square like a knocked-out tooth.
As soon as she stepped into view she'd turn her face

and wave her hand the whole fifteen steps before she disappeared,
with shocking suddenness, obliterated by a wall of brick.
Still, in the vacancy she'd left behind, her hand's white flutter

hung like an afterthought or seam she'd stitched into the air
between this space and the world's fabric that spread beyond,
invisibly, with streetcar stops and shops and other people.

I came to think the house between us had been razed
so we could see each other from this distance:
the child framed by the window with her braids dangling

over the flower box, the woman walking through a drizzle
in her gray coat, making an effort to look cheery and confident
as she turned back to wave, just as the child,

leaning far out over the sill, tried not to give away
that she'd noticed the strain of the gesture. Waving,
she knew then, was a way of measuring absence

and naming its ghosts with signs drawn in the air.
And I remember the rusty springs of an unraveled mattress
exactly halfway in between our hands:

it lay on a pile of ruined brick and cracked concrete,
a witness to our waving and how our motions
made a fabric between its stubborn coils until it was

a bed inside a house with walls where someone dreamed
of a girl and a woman waving across a windswept space,
and suddenly their hands flew toward each other: wings of a white
    bird.

My Mother's Hand Thinks

It lies limp on the sheet as if dropped there,
a pale yellow maple leaf. Fall shakes its branches
through the window. The old lie stretched out
on their beds after the midday meal. *Do you have a home?*

my mother asks through her closed eyes
and through a distance where everything is whirled
off its tethering. To my quick *Yes* she very slowly says,
You're lucky, as if she has to fetch these words

from far away, and then her mind drifts off, not sleeping,
but tossed in its own restless wind.
That's when her hand begins to wake. A rippling first
among the tendons on its wilted back, then the five

fingertips rub against the covers, and, as if touch
is memory, more motion enters. The hand lifts
from the sheet onto my mother's gown. Nervous antennae,
the fingers quiver here and there, until they run into

the stitching of the seam. For a moment, they stop
in recognition, before they sense the first smooth round
of a button, then another, and another up to the first one
by her throat. The thumb, on its side now, circles

the polished rim with the dip at the center. It feels
the loops of threads tethering the button's disk
to the fabric. All is there as it has always been,
with each blouse, each dress, in each house, even

the small nightgowns she wore as a child: always
a row of buttons from the throat down to the waist,
a path to travel, direction, the call of something old and safe.
My mother's hand thinks. Again the slow tip of the thumb

circles over the button's rim; smoother than skin,
more solid than thought, it sits like a door
over its opening. *A door,* the hand thinks, and so,
from underneath the seam, the index finger lifts

the button to a tilt, and the two fingers meet
on each side of the disk, feeling for the hemmed slit
in the fabric, that soft-lipped exit. My mother's hand
undoes the button by her throat.

It holds its index finger over the bottom of the hole
and its thumb over the top. It weighs the hole
between its fingers. It likes this nothing where it meets
itself. It walks its fingers down to the next button

less slowly, less hesitantly now.
There are clear markers. There is a purpose here,
a place it's always known and that,
when all else whirls away, is home.

The Nightgown

Just before it swooped down, from the nurse's skilled hands,
fluff of white folds, weightless from years of laundering,
for a moment my mother held up her arms over her head,
over that poor hunched nakedness. That's when I saw
how the body, old, reaches inside itself,

craving more and more spaces to dwell in: crimped tucks
below the armpits and each rib, drapes smocked below the chin,
across the belly quilted pleats: beds, hollows, nooks,
and nooks. And when the gown swooped down, a fluid un-
folding of a screen, I remembered how she had

opened my own gown over my taut child's trunk,
how I'd raised up skinny arms to receive it
as she received it now. I wanted to hide in those folds:
lithe sun-dried cotton, waves of embrace where the day's
blame was forgiven. Didn't the saints in the books

drape their bodies in endless folds below the gilded halos?
How could I know then that the body as it ages
knits its own garment, thousands of pockets
to hold all it cherished, all it lost, all it had hurt,
once more close to itself. But at the moment

the white seam reached my mother's ankles
and her arms fell into her lap where she sat on her bed,
I heard the deepest sigh, saw it lift itself
from the gown and open into a wide umbrella,
folds and folds and folds of feathery air billowing,

as my mother kept breathing out and out,
releasing, without hesitation, without fear or judgment,
all she had held inside her—

Two Rings

The sunlit reading room where we sit is a room
without books. The very old don't read anymore.
They carry their own plots inside them.

They know them by heart, stories as old
as the heart: they don't want anything new.
Their thoughts are a slow revolving dance,

a ring around what's been. Sister Therese,
in her brown habit, knows this dance. She's the one
who closes their eyes and who

before folding their hands takes off the rings
from their helpless fingers. Sister Therese
holds my mother's wedding band in her palm,

a ring of reddish Russian gold worn thin from sixty years
on my mother's hand. Someone has taped a Band-Aid around it,
a pink flag with her name marked in black ink.

Someone found this ring among her clothes.
But I hold what was sent to me, what
my mother wore at the end, a pale gold, unfamiliar band

Sister had taken herself from my mother's finger.
This is the evidence in the reading room with no books:
two rings and a missing finger:

my mother died with a stranger's ring on her hand.
Someone slipped it on her finger when her own ring
had wiggled itself over the thinning knuckle.

Two golden bands on the fake grain of the Formica tabletop.
Sister Therese pulls her hand back into her sleeve:
You'd better keep them both. And so I leave with two rings

and one story that lacks the gesture by which
they're linked. The heart circles in its old track,
a slow dance around what's missing.

Heart, My Heart

Heart, my heart, convulsed with helpless troubles…
—Archilochus

Listen . . . This is how I want to begin.
But there is no one to listen. The light has dragged itself
away from the shrubs, its fading cloth pulled up
across the garden walls and hills. Only its hem

still slides across the peaks, slowly, a little unraveled
by the sharp rock. Who now will listen?
It matters, this question, that's why it has to be asked
each time again so that what yearns can rise,

so that we can go on like the old poets who invented the *heart,*
took that pink pulsing organ, not out of the body,
but out of its anonymity, its impersonal *it,*
and shaped it into the other, the *you,*

lifting its head in the bloodstream, listening—
They knew that inside this pulsing some ache
takes shape, as when a storm looms, the looming
is not a shape, but a shaping. Oh heart,

you other and not other— A deer steps
from the pines below the hills. Grass bends
under its hooves and the scent
of bruised stalks mixes with this morning's rain.

The fur on the deer's neck is matted from the wet branches
that stroked across its length; ears
turning, then upright and still, trembling just barely . . .
I thought it might be *you,* leaving the thickets for a moment

to take in the fields where I work and grieve.
I had a mother once; I spoke to her
as if she were my heart. She listened and told me
who I was. A child doesn't know about the heart,

taking her doll down the garden path to the pond
where the dragonflies skirt the water. In the stillness
the child talks to the doll, and the words skirt
the porcelain face before the web spun in the senses

trembles in recognition. This is how the child
rehearses being alone. Grasses nod in the wind,
and each leaf on the birches is an ear. The whole world
holds still in the light, not dipped in it,

but holding it up like a silk tent, rocking a little.
Companion, *you* shaped in the blood,
last month I buried my mother's ashes under a birch.
It rained and drops gathered on the leaves and fell

more slowly than the rain: there was such hesitation
in the air that the mourners' umbrellas
balanced fine columns of glass on their black canopies,
like a juggler's act before gravity overcomes it.

This made mourning look like an art. It isn't.
My mother stopped listening when I was six:
grief plugged her ear; the noise of war, nothing else
could enter. It took a while to understand

that when there is no one to listen
a shape in the blood floats up as an ear.
At first I called it *you*. Later I called it *heart,*
for I am not so far removed from Archilochus

and know when the world is *heartless,*
its parents, its politicians, its soldiers, its language,
its plain citizens like myself:
there is an ache, something convulsing

deep inside like muteness, like blindness,
like yearning to hear what's true—
Listen, my heart, the moment you lift yourself
out of the troubled stream I will remember how to begin.

part three

Still Life

Those long hot hours after school, weeding the garden plot,
her sister gone, her mother working in the city, a stillness
crept up from the loosened soil and what had been uprooted.

From where she stooped between thinned seedlings,
she'd hold her breath. Instantly, the birds' voices stopped
and hung in the air, glittering explosions of silky dust.

Then the sun stood still over the cabbage plot, a glowing
cabbage itself, layers and layers of searing heat
over its terrible, invisible heart. Cabbage moths

hovered in one place: little ghosts of children
who had come back to play. The priest next door in his black frock
froze among his chrysanthemums; the coffee grounds he mixed

into the soil to dye the blossoms a darker shade
had slid from his hands, a scattering of blackened crumbs
caught in a draft like thoughts suspended—free

of the need to end their flight. The apples in the orchard
didn't fall; they swam in the air, green constellations
lost in a pool of stillness. It was the heat,

its honeyed light that held them, a light so thick
it canceled all forwards and backwards. Even the ants,
circling the mounds of weeds with their nervous run,

forgot themselves and sat in the dust, chips of polished shell.
Was it this to be dead? This kind of hush,
this drowning in a breathless air?

Then she wouldn't have to be afraid—
She could see each thing stunned in a place
where everything was now and nothing later.

Variations on an Invisible Hand

*The true mystery of the world
is the visible, not the invisible.*
—Oscar Wilde

1

We were cut from the same cloth.
The same designs unfurled inside her.
But she was different. That's why
she was my sister and not myself.
That's why my hand writes this instead of hers.
If her hand told its story it would be one hidden
inside a mitt tied with a ribbon to her wrist.
White cotton knit covered the four fingers,
shapes so sickened and unlike themselves,
only the mitt let them still be, invisibly, fingers.
Except that the thumb with a child's
square nail stuck out from a hemmed opening,
where the cotton made a boundary of stitches
with plain white thread:
the visible stitched to the invisible.

2

Some days while we played my sister cried
without stopping. The saints should have stepped down
from their high windows. It's not the lead
they're fastened with that keeps them from descending.
They know their limits, that the body's suffering
is something given, like stars and crops.
Their watching made the cries rise up like dust
onto the sills. Pain has no limits.

3

At Chartres one late afternoon I watched the light
slant through the windows in radiant fingers as if I'd stepped
into the secret of her mitten. A million specks of dust
climbed in long processions up the transparent shafts.
Whether there was more light or more dust, I couldn't tell.
One drifted freely in the slow currents of the other.
Pain is not shapeless, but a sheer way of knowing.

4

Oh, little thumb, you steeple, keep pointing in the distance,
keep burning, little candle.

5

The blanket I'd spread over the long-stemmed grasses
was spiked with seeds. I carried it home; tiny pointed
pods kept holding on, hard as I shook the fabric.
I spread it out on the kitchen table: behind each needle's point
there was a shaft with furry tufts raised up as barbs.
Like a harpoon each stuck inside the cotton, the tip
protruding on one side, the twisted tail end on the other.
No way to pull them out but through. And as the blanket's weave
had opened, it closed behind them, forgiving—

Beauty is seeing through a thing utterly.
When Hermes, in the story, watched the turtle
cross the yard he saw not just the creature
fleeing from dust into the grasses, but the perfect
half-round of its back already strung with gut and plucked—
friend of the feast he called it,
before his knife cleanly scooped out
the flesh from its shell to make the instrument.

Friend of the feast—it could be anything,
a turtle, a thumb, the long-stemmed grasses—
The Heart wants what it wants . . .
Its spark is pure attention.

6

In one dizzying moment, at the fair,
when I sat next to her and gravity pulled us
close against each other in the tilting seat,
my sister put her hand on my knee.
Just as the tilt-a-whirl accelerated and we screamed,
I saw her thumb was *naked,* and its nakedness
next to the mitten's cloth seemed a strange skin
it had put on to jolt me into seeing it.
I thought of it yesterday, reading in the *OED*
those earliest comparisons using the word:
naked like a worm, —like a needle, or *—like a nail.*
I had to guess what these reversed: the worm in the ground?
the needle in its casing? the nail in wood?
Mystery is in the shock of nakedness,
not in what is hidden.

Two Stories of Your Hand

Mother's came first, *her* story about the flight to Berlin
when the plane went out of control over the lake near the city.
Late summer 1939, and she six months pregnant.
She didn't tell me this until years after you were gone.
I drew you then, curled inside her as she was plummeting
toward earth: how your tiny, still perfectly formed hand
tried to hold on to something, cringe from the approaching lake
toward Mother's racing heart. In this moment of her story,
it was her crazed pulse, the rush of panic's chemicals
that overtook your hand, the clockwork of cells
scrambling their work. She said barely one hundred meters above the
    water
the plane caught itself. In my X-ray vision I drew her veering up
    and up,
but the child was still falling, hitting bottom in its watery balloon,
you, your hand bouncing off the walls with a thud. It began here,
my story of your hand with the rebellious cells
secreting their protest against the world you were to enter,
a world listless in the heat over Werbellin Lake,
over Hermann Göring's hunting lodge, which the pilot had been
    pointing out
to his passengers. You sensed danger in each window,
glaring from the shore, so terrible your hand puffed up,
sending crazed messages into each finger to fester there and spread.
Lost already, you thought you had nothing to lose.
I should have warned you from where I waited on the ground.
When I looked up it was too late. The plane had caught itself.
It did not crash onto the lodge on the shore, nor dive
into the lake. It was going to deliver you into this world without
    pity.

Mazes

—application for citizenship

When the officer took my hand in her rubber glove
I tried to let her have it like a thing
that knew nothing of itself and now was guided
by her purpose. *Relax,* she said between each rolling of a fingertip
from one side to the other, so that
its whole face—ear to ear if fingertips had ears—was printed
inside the green-framed box on the chart.
I looked for myself inside its mazes. Could they show
what brought me here? Whorled lines like narrow back roads
taken by ancestral Huguenots across the Prussian border:
wagons, bundles, Luther's Bible under the seat,
on their breath soon the first guttural sounds adapting their names . . .
At the center of the middle finger, ridges
where the lines, arched and leaning sideways, looped
as if here all roads turned back: families with sons
fleeing Prussian recruiters for land offered free on the Volga;
five generations, then they went packing west again,
stripped of means by Bolsheviks. And here was I,
learning to leave one country for the mazes of another.
Think of them as breath, its balance
between gaining ground and losing it.

New World

The gatekeeper held up her torch.
She looked stern. It was dawn.
The skyline glittered in crisp air. Over a barge
a flock of gulls imploded. Loaded with waste
the grim hulk passed us heading out to sea, as if the city
had scrubbed itself overnight. That day
I'd come to claim a passport stamped with innocence,
so anxious to forget that ravaged continent I'd left,
each year a little more, until I had erased half of myself:
new laws, new friends, new rooms, new speech . . .
How far, I wondered, is *new* from *pure?*
How far is *new* from *whole?*

Last night I read about a man who collected
silence, which he'd record and play to himself
when he despaired of the world's grime and noise:
the hush of dogs worn out from barking
under the moon; a girl lost in thought over her book;
the flutter of eyelids across her field of vision;
bread rising under white cloth . . .
The more he listened the more he heard
the small impurities in his recordings,
tiny scratches, a scampering of mice or ghosts . . .
They drove him mad, finally, but I

could have told him not even
newborns are new. I was one once,
dumped into the grime of history. It sticks
to the first scream you add to the world's blare.
Ask the gulls. They know where newness
ends: they always hesitate a moment,

hovering over the seamless mirror—feet
stretched ahead of themselves, wings tilted
to slow their glide—before they break
the unbroken image.

How else could you land?

Litany without Saints

1. The Thorn

In third grade I watched a boy beat a girl
with a stake he'd yanked from a fence.
He beat her with all the force
of his short arms, his shorn head tipping
back and forth in brisk February wind,
aiming the stake at her stockinged legs,
while they ran side by side as if together
bolting from this moment's terror which froze
in my head: that I hadn't rushed to her side,
hadn't tried to stop this brute fury of muscle
whom the other boys were cheering on,
hadn't walked her home after he'd slowed and let her go.
I saw the stake he'd thrown to the ground,
the rusty nail at its end. In my ears
her scream, still scrambling up to a ledge,
threw itself down, shattering
in jagged bits lodged in me from then on.
Because I'd glimpsed something there
not to be trusted, so chilled
it couldn't move but sat like a thorn in wood.
Hard. Pointed. Evil. How I'd have to live
with knowing I too was not good.

2. The Hand

To get a fresh towel she had to step
onto the edge of the lowest shelf
in that old-fashioned wardrobe in the bedroom,
reach up to where a crack
opened behind the upper shelf by the wardrobe's back,

and pull herself up so that, wedged
between the open doors and half suspended,
she was eye to eye with stacks of washcloths
and folded linens. The air she breathed in there
was not the same she breathed outside,
but clean as if an iron had pressed and singed away
the odor of the world, its oils, its soils, the scent of skin,
the spills, the grime: clean
like a bone stripped of its flesh.
Her eyes strayed deep into the tunnels
between neat cotton stacks in search of the pattern
she favored: white blossoms on a background of blue.
What she saw in the dim interior, halfway between,
halfway behind two walls of terry cloth,
made her stop: a child's hand lay on the shelf,
clean, still, and utterly strange without a body.
It didn't belong to this world of moving things,
the truck outside the window, the clock
ticking from the dresser behind her,
the heart thumping inside the thin walls of her chest.
It was her sister's. The last time she'd seen it
it lay on the sheet below the cuff
of the blue nightgown she now would wear for good.
It had come back, someone had saved it.
It lived in the back of the wardrobe.
The world wasn't as she thought.
There were no boundaries. She reached
and touched the knuckle of that little finger
for a split second. From a great distance
a nerve, a tiny electrical shock,
called to her arm. Then she felt herself
let go of the shelf and stepped
from the dim opening back into daylight
and truck fumes wafting through the window.

3. Tracks

Nights she listens to his breathing. It fills the room
with rustling thickets, stalks the dark,
a soft-pawed, graceful animal looking for a way out.
No matter how carefully she caulks the cracks in the walls
and seals the doors, it finds a way,
senses the draft from a small hole
somewhere in the cinder blocks and gnaws there
for months, for years, until the gap is wide enough.
Then it will leave, not without pressing
its furry cheek against her sleep, not without running
its moist muzzle across her neck. In the morning
tracks will cross the snow of the wide field,
reach to the horizon, then pass over that line
into the sky. Up the hazy ladder it will climb,
up into the palest branches. There it will turn
and look across the buried fields back to the light
inside her window, through eyes that don't remember
anything but snow: endless, frozen sheets.

4. Holding On

Such sickness, this certainty of having failed,
not knowing why or what she could have done:
she'd missed an appointment, though no news
had reached her regarding the place or the assignment.
Some urgent message had denied itself and scattered.
Its sickening absence spread over the house, staring
from snowy sockets into her window, arrived
with the mailman, his bag stuffed with sealed threats; crept
from the feathers of the flicker who'd killed himself
against the windowpane. That day she left the house
and walked into a field of mottled stalks
and crusts of layered frost. Lined up,

like last year's ragged rows of corn, the dead
stood grumbling there: bones, rage, longings, and complaints.
Why is it I who stands here? said one, *and why you
over there?* She shook her head. This was the work,
this holding on to the stripped branches in the wind,
not knowing why you're spared, why one bird sings
on its lonely perch and another flies straight
into a country that shatters in its heart.

5. Song of the Glasses

I know a tremor in my bones, so faint
I only hear it when I'm still, in moments
when the world draws back and I can feel
the hidden point where mind and body
overlap, as if they knew each other
as one single pulse. It's a point
below the region where the throat narrows
like the hollow stem of a champagne glass,
in which the eye, lost in a shining corridor,
suspends its way. Most days the world's
clutter obscures this place and the fine
stirrings that come from there.
I wouldn't know of it except for my mother's
goblets in our hallway cupboard:
wide-rimmed, almost as thin as skin, they sense
the slightest traffic in the house.
Instantly they start to tremble and, brushing
rim to rim, they ring below a whisper.
They stop me in the hallway.
They sing of fragile things, of breaking.
Still, nine of them have lasted
over a hundred years, competing
with the longevity of flesh,

which doesn't shatter, but knows a shudder
as something gives and rips,
though I can't hear it. Instead I am
astonished at the thinness of these glasses,
their frosted flutes like frozen breath,
astonished at the beauty of frailty.

The Cap

For months her view was barred by crusts of snow.
The only marker of the neighbor's garden was the laundry wire
that used to run along the edge of broken soil.
It served as lookout for the sparrows;
it served her eyes to glide along its smooth
black line in search of entries, signs, surprise.
But where it ended on both sides a pole
stood planted in the earth where nothing grew
but dormant turf. And so her eyes went back and forth.
Then it was Easter. The air still crisp,
but bright. The man next door
hung his baseball cap on the laundry wire.
Amazed, her eyes moved round its bright
circumference and could not tell what made
its whiteness different from the snow's fading habits:
was it the fabric's mesh filled with mosaics of spring light,
the perfect hemisphere the old man molded
from the dripping crown, having fastened two pins
to the visor? How the cap swayed
back and forth, caught between thoughts.
How between heaven and earth
it was the point where memory found reason
to contemplate the old man's silvery rim of hair
where the cap left a permanent groove
like the imprint of a halo.
On the wire, the cap's adjustable strap
with its small notches kept waiting to be locked
into the matching holes on the other side
and fitted onto the skull. Such patience.
It knew the thaw had just begun.
Her eyes went round and round the crown's white circle
to mark the place in its depression where soon
his humble head would plot the garden's blessings.

The Dump

We weren't allowed to play there. It was filthy,
my mother sternly said, scrubbing grimy sickles
from under our nails. You could catch polio.

From her lips the *o*'s rolled down into the sink
and floating there took on pale soapy rings
circling the drain before they vanished

down the metal grate into that pit below, black,
bottomless, bleeding always into itself. After lunch
we cuddled our dolls, then drifted beyond the sandbox and the
        swing.

Between weeds our shovels sifted the refuse
for rubble of summer guests from long ago: a battered
spoon with engraved lettering, *Otto* buried under curlicue;

the ornate oval of a picture frame, shards of a mirror
in which we saw our faces puzzled and cracked.
And what we cherished most: those small glass bottles

of vanished medicines with their transparent chambers
in blues and greens intact, sacs of air like little fossilized lungs.
Wiping them with our sleeves and dipping our fingers

into the narrow throats for the last grains of sand,
we lifted them above us into the wind and made them sing,
a voice gathered from back in the pines

with perfectly round lips softly breathing ohhh,
the longest, most patient moan: ohhh for polio,
for summers gone, and ohhh for us and for, oh, everything.

part four

Train

Not evening, not morning, it's that space
in between, a hammock hung from tree to tree
where the sleeper, hardly swaying, is a dead weight

in the wind. In the distance the whistle
sounds twice its long deliberate call,

and the sleeper wakes halfway and wonders
what might have passed unseen and loaded,
one car after another humming along the tracks,

with things she might have held in her own hands
to see if they might change her. Imagine this sleeper

to be a woman who's lived all her life in this town,
where the train passes at night out by the prairie's edge
between sagebrush and dropseed:

for years she's heard its rumbling and turned over
on her pillows, remembering the gravel-filled bed

where as a girl on summer nights she'd watch its taillight
blinking. Two lines going east, two lines going west,
like past and future diverging: oh, she's chased after them,

but it's the present, like breath inside her, that's the most
secret of all. How can she fully wake, though, when her mind

is married to the moon, which turns and turns by its old
jealous laws and cannot stop for fear of falling?
Nothing remains, her mother told her. *I've seen it happen.*

Don't claim what you might lose. She'd asked, *What is it then
that can't be lost?* If there was an answer, she can't remember.

And so each night she vows sometime before she dies
she'll run out and meet that train that always wakes her;
she'll get up and flag it down with a flashlight,

if that's what it takes, if that's what she's always missed.
But once the whistle's sounded she falls asleep again,

dreaming of gourds hung in the barn to dry, ripe and sealed:
seeds rattling their secrets inside them. If only
one would burst and save her.

The Bumblebee

I woke to a huge hum. Had it hatched
from a dream in which the door to an attic
had opened? No, it was caught within the space
between my window and the gauzy curtain:
a furry body buzzed crazily against the glass.
Each time it reached the edge
where the white frame divided the panes
the humming stopped for one long breath
as it rested, dazed, on the wooden ledge,
while the air still trembled with longing
that this sheer contraption give way.
Out there I could see the world waiting and waving:
brambles of blackberries, the plum tree's
weighted branches, clouds crossing a continent.
So much to be tasted, so much to be wanted,
if wanting could wake enough to make its claim,
where so much still was mute, still hesitating
in a room of poisonous spindles like that of the girl
curled on the attic cot, nursing her bloody
finger, which knew that wanting stings.
Then the buzzing started again with new fury.
Its hum was huge. The whole room
ached with it. That's what it took:
you wouldn't know the world
if you didn't want it enough.

Cyrene

Don't ask why divine lovers appear in the disguise
of animals. I had just killed a lion that had been
stalking me, when he emerged from the woods:
wolf of a god or god of a wolf.
Not human, he was both. But it didn't matter:
his eyes were amber and his fur was not too coarse and not
too soft, a splendid pelt to cover my skin
where I wanted it covered.
Deep in my ear I heard his whisper: this
was the shape of pleasure, which doesn't think
but shines in its displays. I wanted only him,

but not as swan or raven or tender
of docile flocks. I wanted my wolf, his quivering
pricked ears to listen to my stories, the roughness
of his tongue that licked the kisses from my mouth.
When he came back dressed in feathers,
I pretended not to know him and left to hunt alone.
The wolf is my true love. Unlike the gods, I have my limitations.

Growing in Spirit

He who hopes to grow in spirit . . .
. . . will not be afraid of the destructive act:
half the house will have to come down.
—C. P. Cavafy

Sometimes after sunset we sit outside until it's dark.
Then your face across the table grows softer in the shadows,
young in the way we once were young, wilder,

not afraid of the *destructive act* the poet praises.
Those mornings I woke and nursed a child
that was yours also, a son as rash as he was beautiful.

Once when I nursed him a magnolia blossom fell at my feet,
each petal bruised, each bruise a night you spent away. Each time
you claimed there was no music left in our house, I watched the
     paint

begin to blister on the walls and fall. But grief makes a strong child:
he grew long graceful limbs, hair like a patch of sunlit oats,
though when he lifted up a stone, bricks crumbled from the chimney.

When he threw a stick, timbers cracked and windows shattered.
When he cried, wind swept inside with a music of salt and rain.
It reached into the basement, didn't leave one thing unturned,

shook beams and bolts until they sang.
Then the child picked up his instrument and played.
Each night the strings trembled under his fingers as we began to
     mend

the walls and fasten the doors onto their hinges.
And when we set the glass back into the window frames,
we did it carefully, sealing his music inside like air

into a collapsed lung. When we looked up at last
the child was grown. Together from the doorstep
we waved until we lost him down the street.

Some nights now something still rattles the panes
and makes us shiver. Then we hold each other
and whisper, remembering the spirit's wages.

Eurydice

They never tell that she had children,
supple as lambs, that she tended a garden
and, when he played his instrument, looked
at her own face in the water pail,

dreamed of those words overheard at the well.
Old women's words, women who kicked
the shards of broken jugs, scarves over skulls
and skin at the mouth gathered with many stitches.

They bent over the stony rim as over an ear,
muttering: how love shatters or slowly chips away,
how beauty washes from a face as easily as chalk
from slate, how children grow and leave.

Each day her listening reached until it yawned,
a cave where she heard nothing else and entered
deep, finding the trail down the steep spiral
into the orifice of night where listening

is all there is and the mind forgets its way back.
And so what did it wasn't, as they like to say,
a small fanged coil sprung from the earth;
it was that she wanted him to remember

her seamless face, their passion unspoiled, her mothering
still sweet like milk before it turns in the night air.
She wanted to live on his lips forever
suspended, a white shell cradled between two waves.

Night Cows

They enter the house after dark
now that the children are gone.

Lying next to my husband, who turns
in his sleep, I hear them:

black bulks shifting in the abandoned rooms,
their mournful mooing so low I have to lift my head

to know no one is calling for me through the long hours.
Their moist jaws work the dark, turning it over

on rough powerful tongues, all night
chewing it, filling their four cavities

with the black broth—gone, gone, gone,
and gone, they say, and muffled voices answer

from hidden catacombs where mothers
bury the craft of their mothering.

And just before dawn—their bodies plump and huge
as if the black air had nourished them and thinned

around the house—before my husband wakes,
they've ambled back outside into the snow.

At breakfast I see them in the pasture across the road,
the field white and glistening, and they

scattered and motionless: a charred urn
exploded on bleached cloth.

Erigone

Of all the women who ascended to the heavens,
Erigone was the poorest . . . the beggar . . . orphan . . .
the death that is not assimilated back into life . . .
that wanders about continually in the air, with the spirits
of the dead, the dolls and masks hung from a tree.
—Roberto Calasso

First I heard the dog whimper. Then I knew
what I would find: the corpse under the tree,
its dear gray hair; knew I'd always be a beggar,
a child who wants the only thing it cannot have.
The wind came by on his wide sled. He slithered
through my hair, seducer of deserted spaces,
he knew a beggar is not choosy and lives off air.
I let him slither between my legs, I tried
to compromise. The tree watched us.
It had a thousand arms. Someday, I knew,
I'd need them: such tenderness beneath the foliage,
such secrets in its acorns. First I waited to see
what was inside them. Then I never left.
This is the mystery: there is a world out there
that stretches out of sight with many trees,
with many men, but nothing could entice me
to follow them. Who planted this acorn
in my chest? My father would have told me
mysteries have but one law which is not to be understood.
There's a gap between the question and the answer,
the space where you suspend yourself for lack
of a geography. A beggar might as well embrace
the alms she gets. So I climbed up into the many branches,
the noose already dangling from my neck.
It came with the tree. But don't we hang, each one of us,

on some strange thread we did not choose
but that chose us? How it pulls at the limbs
and makes us dance and jerk. Don't think I hang alone here.
I have your company in the tree's dark chandelier.
Some trees bear fruit, some trees bear corpses.
Don't you see they are the same?

Helen

When he first came, I didn't run
with the screaming maids, I dropped
my needle and then my husband's shirt
in the orchard of olives where I
had been waiting. On his boat at first
I didn't speak. I don't speak well;
my tongue is a root anchored in stone.
He took me then on the furs
under the cedar deck, but I
wanted to be taken, not because his limbs
were handsome like a god's, but because
to be desired makes beauty what it is,
not useful, but complete. What would I have been
without a city burning, a girl under a tree
sewing her husband's shirt? I wanted
to know desire, its singe, but all I knew then
was being wanted, as if there were
no man I could love, only the story of the self
burning within its broken walls:
a queen surrounded by her ring of maids;
the hero lunging through the gate; woman is woman
by spending her maidenhood.
Let the city fall. Tell them the ring of truth
is the ring of beauty: one takes down the walls,
the other lights up what vanishes.

2

After sunrise, for years, I would climb up
the parapet and watch the spectacle.
What else was there to do

while my new husband polished his armor
for the next round. Shields gleamed on the plain
like plates stacked upright in a rack.
The gods took their positions on distant peaks
or hidden in the crowds—not that I
could see them, but I knew, being a pawn myself
in their cruel games. They can't die,
so they're fascinated to watch us.
Death is a miracle to them, they do not
tire of watching it over and over again:
the utter stillness, the refusal to ever wake,
the release of the limbs, the wide-open
stare that sees nothing, the wide-open mouth
that says nothing. They cannot get
enough of this nothing. They cannot touch it,
like a hole in the fine quilt of their designs.
Everything is something, they argue, how
can it be less? Nights I stand by the mirror
and open my braids. I shake out my hair
and watch the ashes fall from it like gnats,
clouds of them drifting to the ground:
dust from the funeral pyres, skin and flesh
dissolved into black flour.

3

I didn't get to die. They spare someone
to do the mourning, to regret, to age.
One day instead of dimples I found lines,
then hair turned silver. Widowed,
I heard their sneers above me in the wind.
The body moves inside itself to tend
what never bloomed, seeds that fell into the cracks.
Even the flower of sex moves deeper
between the ruined walls, its roots so keen

they reach a well beyond the crumbling gate.
And there he stood, the one who had been waiting.
In mourning everything is simple: together
you enter a city without walls,
lament in every house, each door a mouth telling
what has been lost, on each stoop a figure
stretching out empty arms until emptiness and emptiness
meet in a ring, of arms, of words
passed patiently around small cooking fires.

The Patience of Ice

What comes after passion? After the walls
around the self go up in flames

like that old city in the story? Fire,
then ice: both belong to the earth,

as passion and patience share the same root,
pati—to suffer, to endure. Today I read

about a man whose body was found in the Alps.
Face cradled on his arm he'd lain there

for five thousand years, berries and quiver
by his side, his ribs still neatly tucked

under the parched canvas of skin, his spine
a knobbly ridge with even markings of a dark dye.

In the picture taken by two hikers
he lies half on the glacier ice and, from his thighs down,

still submerged in slush and icy water,
bald, bony, clay colored. Like the larva of a strange

insect, he tried to climb ashore into the world
of air and time, of mold and microbe,

into the slime of decline, to claim his due,
his proper unraveling. I don't know

what touched me, the curve of his slender back
which must have pearled with sweat of passion once

or his arm's soothing gesture—I think it was
his waiting as he lay there on the ice, facedown,

as if overcome with grief, grief become time
and time *pati,* suffering. I saw how passion

once made him climb and hunt among so many peaks
that he grew weary and longed to calm his pulse and breath,

wished for the sun to rock between two pines
like a round child in an old woman's lap, wished

for one long single breath, a reservoir so deep
he could exhale all longing, that steady hollow ache,

as he lay down to teach his heart
the long white patience of the ice.

His waiting took on the color of glaciers, grew
wide and furrowed as the frozen walls

and with as many chambers, pockets of time unspent,
and suffering imploded like cracks that blossom

inside glass. And so I came to see his patience
in the patience of a child, waiting nine months in the womb

until its lungs unfold to suck the passionate air,
hands ready to grasp. Or in the patience

of the old, waiting on a bench in the park,
hands in their laps. Hours of their hands

holding nothing but air and their eyes shifting
in a small circle that grows closer around them

like a wide cloak so that the cold will take them
not unprepared. Or the patience of our dead,

frozen in the deep cracks where the mind sleeps,
yawns, melts, freezes over and melts again, how

they keep coming back, slowly, steadily, their waiting
immense in its blue-shadowed whiteness,

how they stretch their white hands toward us,
who burn and learn the age-old patience of the ice,

stretch toward us with their blind eyes,
blessing all that endures, forever blessing it.

source notes

"My Mother's Hair"

The complete source for the epigraph is Sherwin B. Nuland's *How We Die: Reflections on Life's Final Chapter* (New York: Knopf, 1994).

"Heart, My Heart"

The epigraph is quoted from Bruno Snell's *The Discovery of the Mind: The Greek Origins of European Thought,* translated by T. G. Rosenmeyer (New York: Harper and Row, 1960).

"Variations on an Invisible Hand"

The source for the reference to Hermes is Karl Kerényi as quoted in Murray Stein's *In Midlife: A Jungian Perspective* (Dallas: Spring Publications, 1983). The phrase "friend of the feast" comes from the Homeric *Hymn to Hermes.* The quotation "The Heart wants what it wants" is from a letter by Emily Dickinson (262, spring 1862) to Mrs. Samuel Bowles: "The Heart wants what / it wants—or else / it does not care—."

"Cyrene" and "Erigone"

I am indebted to Roberto Calasso's *The Marriage of Cadmus and Harmony,* translated from the Italian by Tim Parks (New York: Knopf, 1993), as the source for the mythological background in these poems.

"Growing in Spirit"

I am obliged to C. P. Cavafy's 1903 poem "Growing in Spirit," which begins: "He who hopes to grow in spirit / will have to transcend obedience and respect. / He will hold to some laws / but he will mostly violate . . . / the established, inadequate norm." It ends with these lines: "Sensual pleasures will have much to teach him. / He will not be afraid of the destructive act: / half the house will have to come down. / This way he will grow virtuously into wisdom." Quoted from the revised edition of C. P. Cavafy's *Collected Poems,* translated from the Greek by Edmund Keeley and Philip Sherrard and edited by George Savidis (Princeton, N.J.: Princeton University Press, 1992).